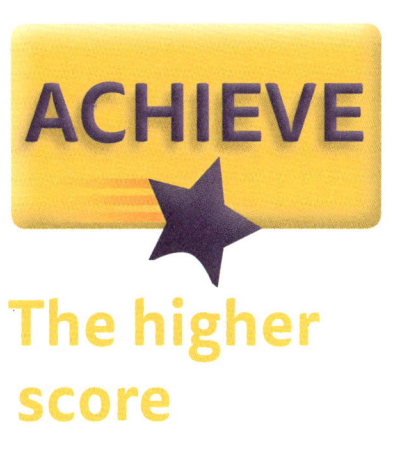

ACHIEVE

The higher score

6

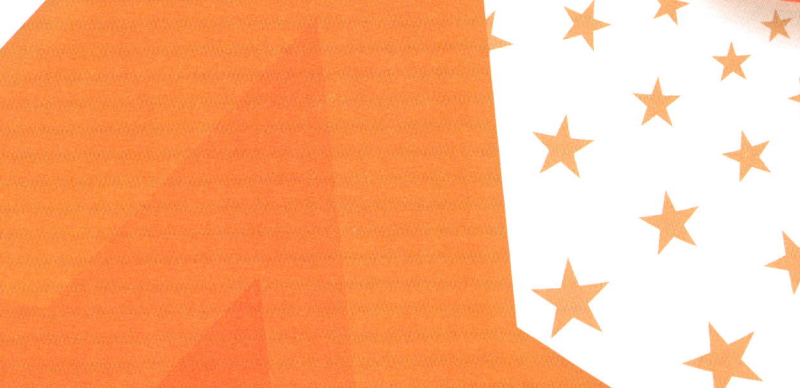

Grammar, Spelling and Punctuation

SATs Revision

Marie Lallaway
& Madeleine Barnes

RISING STARS

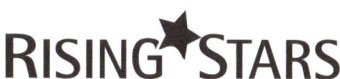

Although every effort has been made to ensure that website addresses are correct at time of going to press, Rising Stars cannot be held responsible for the content of any website mentioned in this book. It is sometimes possible to find a relocated web page by typing in the address of the home page for a website in the URL window of your browser.

Hachette UK's policy is to use papers that are natural, renewable and recyclable products and made from wood grown in sustainable forests. The logging and manufacturing processes are expected to conform to the environmental regulations of the country of origin.

Orders: please contact Bookpoint Ltd, 130 Park Drive, Milton Park, Abingdon, Oxon OX14 4SE. Telephone: (44) 01235 400555. Email: primary@bookpoint.co.uk.

Lines are open from 9 a.m. to 5 p.m., Monday to Saturday, with a 24-hour message answering service. Visit our website at www.risingstars-uk.com for details of the full range of Rising Stars publications.

Online support and queries email: onlinesupport@risingstars-uk.com

ISBN: 978 1 51044 285 6

© Hodder & Stoughton Ltd. (for its Rising Stars imprint) 2019

This edition published in 2018 by Rising Stars, part of Hodder & Stoughton Ltd.
First published in 2015 by Rising Stars, part of Hodder & Stoughton Ltd.
Rising Stars, part of Hodder Education Group
An Hachette UK Company
Carmelite House
50 Victoria Embankment
London EC4Y 0DZ

www.risingstars-uk.com

Impression number 10 9 8 7 6 5 4 3 2 1

Year 2022 2021 2020 2019 2018

All rights reserved. Apart from any use permitted under UK copyright law, no part of this publication may be reproduced or transmitted in any form or by any means, electronic or mechanical, including photocopying and recording, or held within any information storage and retrieval system, without permission in writing from the publisher or under licence from the Copyright Licensing Agency Limited. Further details of such licences (for reprographic reproduction) may be obtained from the Copyright Licensing Agency Limited, https://www.cla.co.uk/

Authors: Marie Lallaway and Madeleine Barnes

Series Editor: Madeleine Barnes

Accessibility Reviewer: Vivien Kilburn

Educational Adviser: Josh Lury

Cover design: Burville-Riley Partnership

Illustrations by QBS Learning

Typeset in India

Printed in Slovenia

A catalogue record for this title is available from the British Library.

Contents

Introduction ... 4
How to use this book ... 6

Grammar

Nouns ... 8
Adjectives ... 9
Adverbs ... 10
Modal verbs ... 11
Adverbials ... 12
Pronouns ... 14
Prepositions ... 16
Determiners ... 18
Subordinating and coordinating conjunctions ... 20
Main clauses and subordinate clauses ... 22
Relative clauses ... 24
Noun phrases ... 26
Subject and object ... 27
Subject and verb agreement ... 28
Verbs in the progressive and perfect tenses ... 30
Passive and active voices ... 32
Subjunctive verb forms ... 34
Standard English and formality ... 36

Punctuation

Capital letters, full stops, exclamation marks and question marks ... 38
Commas ... 40
Inverted commas ... 42
Apostrophes ... 44
Parenthesis ... 46
Colons, semi-colons, single dashes, hyphens and bullet points ... 47

Spelling

Prefixes and suffixes ... 48
Prefixes ... 49
Suffixes: -tion, -ssion, -cian ... 50
Suffixes: -ous, -tious, -cious ... 51
Suffixes: -able, -ably, -ible, -ibly ... 52
Suffixes: -ant, -ance, -ancy, -ent, -ence, -ency ... 53
Words with *ei, eigh, ey, ay* ... 54
Words with *ie, ei* ... 54
Words with *ough* ... 55
Word endings: al, el, il, le ... 56
Silent letters ... 57
Homophones ... 58
Synonyms and antonyms ... 59
Word families ... 60

Word list for Years 5 and 6 ... 61
Glossary ... 62
Answers ... 63

INTRODUCTION

Welcome to Achieve GPS: The Higher Score – Revision

Well done for completing *Achieve GPS: The Expected Standard* revision book, revising everything you need to achieve the expected standard in the Key Stage 2 English Grammar, Punctuation and Spelling (GPS) tests. You are now ready for the next step. In this book you will find key information and activities for more practice and to help you achieve the higher score. You will look again at some of the key knowledge that was in *Achieve the Expected Standard*, but you will use it to tackle trickier questions and apply it in more complex ways.

About the Key Stage 2 Grammar, Punctuation and Spelling National Tests

The tests will take place in the summer term in Year 6. They will be done in your school and will be marked by examiners – not by your teacher.

The tests are divided into two papers:

Paper 1: questions – 45 minutes (50 marks)

- You will answer short questions about grammar, punctuation and language strategies.
- Some questions will ask you to tick a box, circle or underline. Other questions will ask you to add words to a sentence, or to rewrite it making a change. You may be asked to explain why a sentence is written in a particular way.
- The questions will include the language of grammar and punctuation.
- Most questions are worth 1 mark, but you should check to make sure before you answer each question, in case you need to give more than one answer.
- Spelling counts for questions that test tenses, plurals, suffixes and contractions.

INTRODUCTION

Paper 2: spelling – approximately 15 minutes (20 marks)

Twenty sentences will be read aloud to you, one at a time. You will be asked to spell a particular word in each sentence. Some words may require a correctly placed apostrophe.

- The words may be taken from the word lists for Years 1–6.
- Each correct answer is worth 1 mark.

Test techniques

Before the tests
- Try to revise little and often, rather than in long sessions.
- Choose a time of day when you are not tired or hungry.
- Choose somewhere quiet so you can focus.
- Revise with a friend. You can encourage and learn from each other.
- Read the 'Top tips' throughout this book to remind you of important points in answering test questions.
- Make sure that you know what the words in the glossary mean.

During the tests
- READ THE QUESTION AND READ IT AGAIN.
- If you find a question difficult to answer, move on; you can always come back to it later.
- Always answer a multiple-choice question. If you really can't work out an answer, read the question again and try to think of the most sensible response.
- Read the question again after you have answered it. Check you have done what the question asked you to do.
- If you have any time left at the end, go back to the questions you have missed.

Where to get help:

- Page 62 contains a glossary to help you understand key terms about grammar, punctuation and spelling.
- Pages 63–64 provide the answers to the 'Try this' questions.
- Inside back cover contains a revision checklist to help you keep track of your progress.

How to use this book

1 *Introduction* – This introduces each question strand. Each strand has been broken down into smaller strands to help you. Words in bold can be found at the back of the book in the glossary.

2 *What you need to know* – Important facts are given in this section. Read them carefully. Words in bold are key words and those in purple are also defined in the glossary at the back of the book.

3 *Let's practise* – This gives an example question for you to read through. Follow the steps carefully and work through the example.

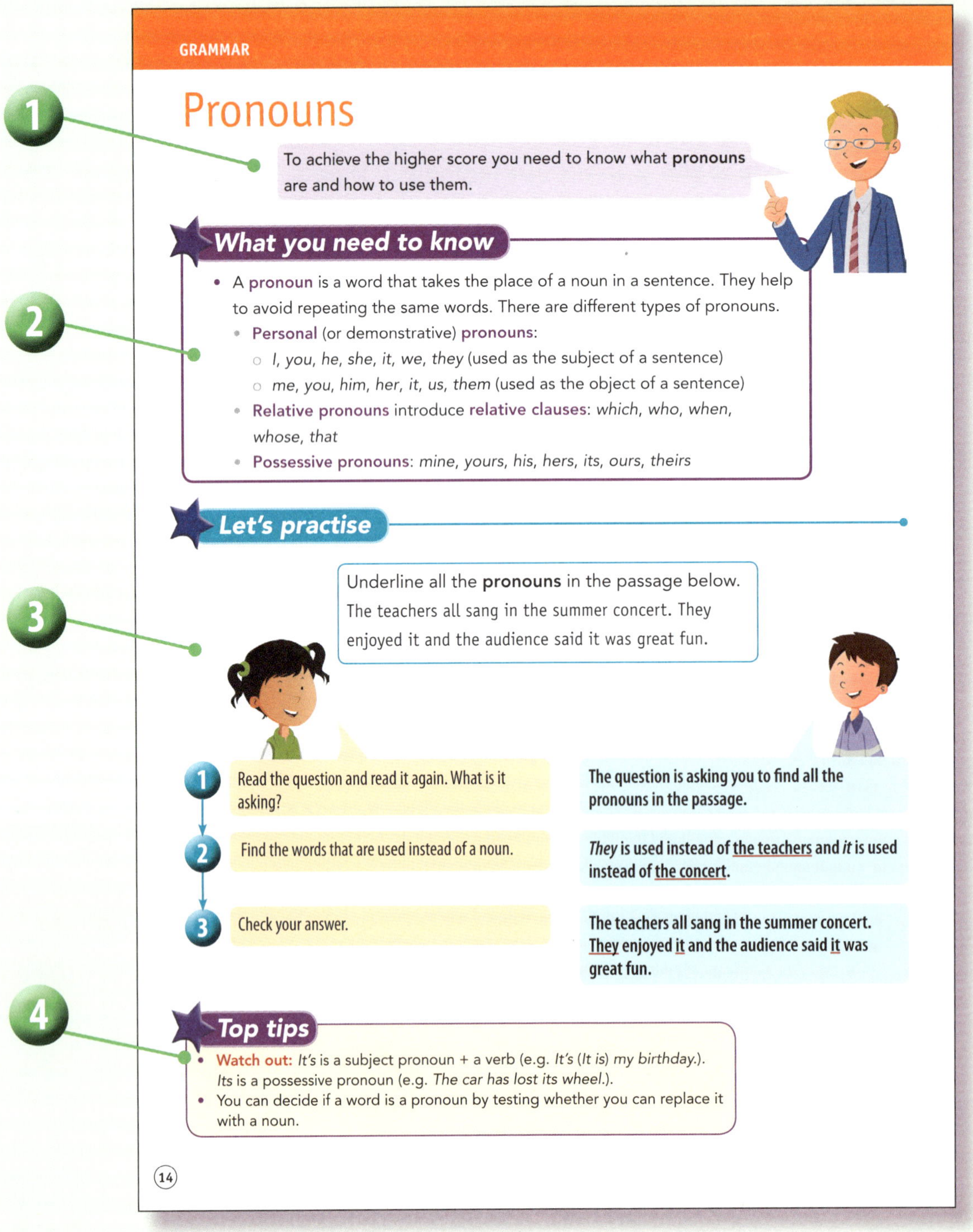

GRAMMAR

Pronouns

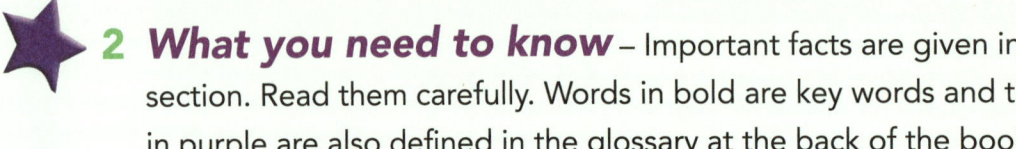

To achieve the higher score you need to know what **pronouns** are and how to use them.

What you need to know

- A **pronoun** is a word that takes the place of a noun in a sentence. They help to avoid repeating the same words. There are different types of pronouns.
  - **Personal** (or demonstrative) **pronouns**:
    - *I, you, he, she, it, we, they* (used as the subject of a sentence)
    - *me, you, him, her, it, us, them* (used as the object of a sentence)
  - **Relative pronouns** introduce **relative clauses**: *which, who, when, whose, that*
  - **Possessive pronouns**: *mine, yours, his, hers, its, ours, theirs*

Let's practise

Underline all the **pronouns** in the passage below.
The teachers all sang in the summer concert. They enjoyed it and the audience said it was great fun.

1	Read the question and read it again. What is it asking?	The question is asking you to find all the pronouns in the passage.
2	Find the words that are used instead of a noun.	*They* is used instead of <u>the teachers</u> and *it* is used instead of <u>the concert</u>.
3	Check your answer.	The teachers all sang in the summer concert. <u>They</u> enjoyed <u>it</u> and the audience said <u>it</u> was great fun.

Top tips

- **Watch out:** *It's* is a subject pronoun + a verb (e.g. *It's (It is) my birthday.*). *Its* is a possessive pronoun (e.g. *The car has lost its wheel.*).
- You can decide if a word is a pronoun by testing whether you can replace it with a noun.

(14)

6

HOW TO USE THIS BOOK

 **4 Top tips** – These hints help you to do your best. Use them well.

 **5 Try this** – Practise answering the questions for yourself.

 **Notebook** – Use a notebook or a piece of paper.

GRAMMAR

Try this

5

1 Tick ✔ one box in each row to show whether the sentences contain **pronouns**.

Sentence	Pronoun	No pronoun
Mr White was tidying his classroom.		
I can't believe that he won.		
The children were playing outside.		
Their kittens were asleep in the bed.		

2 Tick ✔ one box in each row to show the type of **pronoun** used in each sentence.

Sentence	Personal	Possessive	Relative
Where is mine?			
Jane, who was the oldest, took care of everyone.			
She didn't believe the story.			

3 Circle all the **pronouns** in this passage.

I packed our lunchboxes and put them in the car. My mum asked if I had remembered my sandwiches and her flask of tea.

4 Rewrite the sentence below using two **pronouns**. Remember to punctuate your answer correctly.

Simon went to Anna's house.

_____

5 Tick ✔ one box to show the **pronouns** that complete the sentence below.

While I was walking the puppy, ____ was pulling on ____ lead and ____ arm was hurting.

Tick **one**.

I	it's	my	☐
he	her	I	☐
it	its	my	☐
she	my	her	☐

6 Explain why the underlined **pronoun** is used in the passage below.

Jessica was late for school. <u>She</u> had overslept.

_____

15

7

GRAMMAR

Nouns

To achieve the higher score, you need to know what **nouns** are and how to use them.

What you need to know

- There are different types of **nouns** such as proper nouns (names), collective nouns (groups, e.g. *herd*, *flock*), common nouns (for most objects) and **abstract nouns** (for things other than objects).
- Abstract nouns are used for an idea or feeling (e.g. *honesty, jealousy, beauty, thoughts, ideas*).

Let's practise

Circle all the **nouns** in the sentence below.
Whenever Sam and his dog come to visit, the house is filled with excitement.

1 Read the question and read it again. What is it asking?

The question is asking you to identify the nouns in the sentence.

2 Check for proper nouns.

Proper nouns will be the name of something so they have a capital letter. Circle *Sam*.

3 Now check for common nouns and abstract nouns.

Dog and *house* are both common nouns. Circle them. *Excitement* refers to a feeling. It is an abstract noun. Circle it.

4 Check your answer. Have you circled **all** the nouns?

Whenever (Sam) and his (dog) come to visit, the (house) is filled with (excitement).

Try this

1. Circle an **abstract noun** in the sentence below.
   Hannah has a lot of ideas.

2. Rewrite the sentence below, changing the **noun** to create another sentence that makes sense. Remember to punctuate your answer correctly.
   I think your suggestion is absolutely excellent.

Top tips

- **Watch out:** Look out for adjectives that are similar to abstract nouns (e.g. *anger* and *angry*).
- Check to see if an abstract noun makes sense by putting *the* in front of it (e.g. *the anger, the excitement*).

8

GRAMMAR

Adjectives

To achieve the higher score, you need to know what **adjectives** are and how to use them.

What you need to know

- **Adjectives** describe nouns. They may be in front of the noun (e.g. a *hungry* dog), or follow the verb *be* (e.g. the dog *is* hungry).
- Some words can be both adjectives and nouns, **verbs** or **adverbs**. You need to understand what they are doing in a sentence (e.g. He is a *fast* runner – *fast* is used as an adjective; I can run *fast* – *fast* is used as an adverb).

Let's practise

Tick ✓ the box to show which sentence below uses <u>buried</u> as an **adjective**.

The dog <u>buried</u> its bone beneath the bench. ☐
We found <u>buried</u> treasure when we were digging. ☐

1 Read the question and read it again. What is it asking?

The question is asking you to recognise when a word is used as an adjective.

2 Identify the nouns in the sentences.

In the first sentence, *dog*, *bone* and *bench* are nouns. In the second sentence, *treasure* is the noun.

3 Check whether *buried* describes a noun in each sentence.

In the first sentence, *buried* is a verb to tell what the dog did. In the second sentence, *buried* describes the treasure, so it is an adjective. Tick the box for this sentence.

Try this

1 Circle all the **adjectives** in the sentence below.

Sam's table was a mess of sticky glitter, spilled paint and trails of runny glue which trickled onto the floor, but he was happy with the picture he had created.

2 Rewrite the sentence below changing all the **adjectives** to create a new sentence that describes the team as successful. Remember to punctuate your answer correctly.

The team wore disappointed looks because they had gained last place in the competition.

Top tip

- Decide what a word is doing in a sentence before deciding if it is an adjective.

GRAMMAR

Adverbs

To achieve the higher score, you need to know what **adverbs** are and how to use them.

⭐ What you need to know

- Adverbs are used to describe verbs (e.g. Max will leave *soon*).
- Adverbs can appear before a verb, adjective or another adverb, after a verb, or at the beginning or end of the sentence.
- Most *how* adverbs end in *-ly* but not all. Look out for examples such as work *hard*, run *fast*, drive *straight*.
- Adverbs can be used to describe time, place, manner and frequency.

⭐ Let's practise

Underline all the **adverbs** in the sentence below.
Jessica is walking home for tea now.

1 Read the question and read it again. What is it asking?

The question is asking you to find all the adverbs.

2 First, identify the verb.

The verb is *walking*.

3 Check whether any words tell you when, where or how the verb is done.

now = when, *home* = where

4 Check that the other words do not answer the question.

Jessica is walking <u>home</u> for tea <u>now</u>.

✏️ Try this

1 Rewrite the sentence below, changing the **adverb** for another that makes sense. Remember to punctuate your answer correctly.

If you talk too fast, the audience will not understand.

_____

2 Circle all the **adverbs** in the passage below.

We will be home soon. When we get there, you will need to go straight to bed because you've worked hard today.

⭐ Top tip

- **Watch out:** Don't miss common adverbs that refer to *when* something happens: *after, before, later, now, soon, yet.*

10

GRAMMAR

Modal verbs

To achieve the higher score, you need to know what **modal verbs** are and how to use them to show possibility.

⭐ What you need to know

- A **modal verb** is a word that tells you how certain, possible or necessary, an action is: *will, can, could, may, might*.
- A modal verb is used together with another verb (e.g. He *can* run. She *might* win.).

⭐ Let's practise

Tick ✔ one box to show the sentence which describes the action that is **most likely** to happen.

Anna could show you how to do it. ☐
We might have fish and chips for lunch. ☐
Alex will take his pictures home today. ☐
Archie can come to play after school. ☐

1 Read the question and read it again. What is it asking?

The question is asking you to identify which of these events is most likely to happen. You can do this by comparing the modal verbs.

2 Find the modal verbs from each sentence so you are ready to compare them.

They are *could, might, will, can*.

3 Find the sentences which show the actions that will be least likely to happen.

The modal verbs *might* and *could* show the actions that are least likely to happen. *Can* also indicates that the action is not definite.

4 The remaining modal verb is *will*.

Will indicates that an action will definitely happen.

5 Check your answer.

Alex will take his pictures home today.

✏️ Try this

1 Rewrite the sentence below, changing the **modal verb** to make the action more likely to happen. Remember to punctuate your answer correctly.

He might win the race today.

_____

2 Add a **modal verb** to the sentence below to show that the action is possible, not certain.

I _____ be able to fix your phone for you.

(11)

GRAMMAR

Adverbials

To achieve the higher score, you need to identify and construct **adverbials**.

What you need to know

- An **adverbial** is a phrase or clause that tells us more about the verb. It tells us how, when, where or why an action is done. An adverb can be an adverbial, but an adverbial can also be a whole phrase.
- A **fronted adverbial** is often followed by a **comma**, for example: 'Yesterday,'.

Let's practise

Rewrite the sentence below so that it begins with the **adverbial**.

The singers were all smiling after the concert.

1 Read the question and read it again. What is it asking?

The question is asking you to do two things: find the adverbial phrase and move it to the beginning of the sentence.

2 Find the verb.

Were smiling is the verb.

3 Check if there is any information about the verb. Does the sentence tell you how, when, where, or why, the singers *were smiling*?

After the concert tells you *when* they were smiling. This is the adverbial.

4 Rewrite the sentence putting the adverbial at the beginning. Remember to add a comma after the adverbial when it begins the sentence.

After the concert, the singers were all smiling.

5 Check your answer.

Top tips

- *How? When? Where? Why?* Use the same method each time so that you don't forget any of the questions to ask about the verb.
- If an adverbial begins a sentence, it is followed by a comma.

GRAMMAR

 **Try this**

1 Circle the **adverbial phrase** in the sentence below.

A herd of elephants was bathing in the river.

2 Tick ✔ the boxes to show which of the sentences below contain **adverbials**.

Before the start of the film, let's get some popcorn. ☐

I'll give you some money to buy ice-creams for everyone. ☐

I would like a lovely new bicycle. ☐

Mr Carter will come to collect the parcels. ☐

3 Add a suitable **adverbial** to complete the sentence below.

The school football team practises _____.

4 Reorder the sentence below so that it has an **adverbial** at the start of the sentence. Remember to use correct capital letters and punctuation.

Aisling brushed her teeth before going to the dentist.

_____

5 Explain the function of the underlined **adverbial** in the sentence below.

Callum enjoyed the party <u>at Josh's house</u>.

_____

6 Tick ✔ the boxes to show which of the sentences below contain **adverbials**.

The class would go bug-hunting in the woods after lunch. ☐

Please put the books on the table before you leave. ☐

Can I offer you some assistance? ☐

Would you like a drink before supper? ☐

13

GRAMMAR

Pronouns

To achieve the higher score, you need to know what **pronouns** are and how to use them.

⭐ What you need to know

- A **pronoun** is a word that takes the place of a noun in a sentence. They help to avoid repeating the same words. There are different types of pronouns.
  - **Personal** (or demonstrative) **pronouns**:
    - *I, you, he, she, it, we, they* (used as the subject of a sentence)
    - *me, you, him, her, it, us, them* (used as the object of a sentence)
  - **Relative pronouns** introduce **relative clauses**: *which, who, when, whose, that*
  - **Possessive pronouns**: *mine, yours, his, hers, its, ours, theirs*

⭐ Let's practise

Underline all the **pronouns** in the passage below.
The teachers all sang in the summer concert. They enjoyed it and the audience said it was great fun.

1	Read the question and read it again. What is it asking?	The question is asking you to find all the pronouns in the passage.
2	Find the words that are used instead of a noun.	*They* is used instead of <u>the teachers</u> and *it* is used instead of <u>the concert</u>.
3	Check your answer.	The teachers all sang in the summer concert. <u>They</u> enjoyed <u>it</u> and the audience said <u>it</u> was great fun.

⭐ Top tips

- **Watch out:** *It's* is a subject pronoun + a verb (e.g. *It's (It is) my birthday.*). *Its* is a possessive pronoun (e.g. *The car has lost its wheel.*).
- You can decide if a word is a pronoun by testing whether you can replace it with a noun.

GRAMMAR

 Try this

1 Tick ✔ one box in each row to show whether the sentences contain **pronouns**.

Sentence	Pronoun	No pronoun
Mr White was tidying his classroom.		
I can't believe that he won.		
The children were playing outside.		
Their kittens were asleep in the bed.		

2 Tick ✔ one box in each row to show the type of **pronoun** used in each sentence.

Sentence	Personal	Possessive	Relative
Where is mine?			
Jane, who was the oldest, took care of everyone.			
She didn't believe the story.			

3 Circle all the **pronouns** in this passage.

I packed our lunchboxes and put them in the car. My mum asked if I had remembered my sandwiches and her flask of tea.

4 Rewrite the sentence below using two **pronouns**. Remember to punctuate your answer correctly.

Simon went to Anna's house.

_____

5 Tick ✔ one box to show the **pronouns** that complete the sentence below.

While I was walking the puppy, ____ was pulling on ____ lead and ____ arm was hurting.

Tick **one**.

I	it's	my	☐
he	her	I	☐
it	its	my	☐
she	my	her	☐

6 Explain why the underlined **pronoun** is used in the passage below.

Jessica was late for school. <u>She</u> had overslept.

_____

15

GRAMMAR

Prepositions

To achieve the higher score, you need to know what **prepositions** are and be able to use them.

⭐ What you need to know

- A **preposition** is a word that often gives information about time or place.
- The different types of preposition are:
  - Prepositions of time: *after, at, before, by, for, to, until*
  - Prepositions of place: *at, above, by, between, beside, from, in, into, onto, next to, through*
  - Other common prepositions: *of, for, off*
- A preposition introduces a **noun phrase**, which does not contain a verb (e.g. *on* the table, *behind* a damaged statue).

⭐ Let's practise

Tick ✔ one box to show the sentence in which <u>until</u> is used as a **preposition**.

Tick **one**.

We played in the park <u>until</u> it became dark. ☐
School will be open <u>until</u> 7.00 in the evening. ☐
You can stay up <u>until</u> Mum comes home. ☐

1 Read the question and read it again. What is it asking?

The question is asking you to decide which sentence uses *until* as a preposition.

2 A conjunction introduces a clause, which contains a verb. A preposition introduces a noun phrase; this does not contain a verb.
Is *until* followed by a verb or by a noun?

In the first and third sentences <u>until</u> is followed by a verb: *became* and *comes*. In the second sentence, <u>until</u> introduces a noun phrase: *the evening*, so this sentence uses <u>until</u> as a preposition.

3 Check your answer.

School will be open <u>until</u> 7.00 in the evening. ✔

⭐ Top tip

- **Watch out:** Some words can be used as both prepositions and conjunctions: *before, after, until*.

16

GRAMMAR

 **Try this**

1 Underline all the **prepositions** in the passage below.

   I found a feather beneath a tree in the garden. There was a nest perched between the branches.

2 Tick ✔ one box in each row to show whether the word <u>before</u> is used as a **preposition** or as a **subordinating conjunction**.

Sentence	Subordinating conjunction	Preposition
We left the restaurant <u>before</u> dessert.		
Tickets to enter the theme park are more expensive <u>before</u> 11 in the morning.		
We have breakfast <u>before</u> we leave for school.		

3 Add suitable **prepositions** to the sentence below. Use each preposition only once.

   _____ dinner, I put my work _____ the table and began to write _____ my notebook.

4 Rewrite the sentence below, changing the **preposition**. Remember to punctuate your answer correctly.

   Oscar placed the package on the table.

   _____

5 Complete the sentence below with **prepositions** from the box. Use each preposition only once.

   | on   between   beside   opposite |

   The library is _____ the supermarket and the newsagent. It is _____ the bookshop, which is _____ the café _____ the corner.

GRAMMAR

Determiners

To achieve the higher score, you need to know what **determiners** are and how to use them.

⭐ What you need to know

- A **determiner** is a word that shows whether you are referring to a noun in general or in particular. It usually comes at the beginning of a noun phrase.
- There are lots of different determiners but the ones you need to know are:
  - *a* words: *a, an, any*
  - *th* words: *the, that, this, these, those, their*
  - quantity words: *all, some, any, much, more, many, three*
  - possessive determiners: *my, your, her, their*

⭐ Let's practise

> Tick ✔ the sentence that uses the word <u>those</u> as a **determiner**.
>
> I don't like my shoes; I prefer <u>those</u>. ☐
>
> I would love a bag of <u>those</u> sweets. ☐

1 Read the question and read it again. What is it asking?

The question is asking you to identify which sentence uses the word *those* as a determiner.

2 First, look for the nouns. A determiner is used at the beginning of a noun phrase.

In the first sentence, *shoes* is a noun, but it is not used with *those*. In the second sentence, *sweets* is a noun and *those* is used in front of it.

3 Check how *those* is used in the other example.

Those is used to refer to another pair of shoes so it is a pronoun. Therefore, it cannot be the answer.

4 Check you have ticked the correct box.

I would love a bag of <u>those</u> sweets.

⭐ Top tips

- **Watch out:** Some words can be pronouns and determiners. A determiner is used before a noun phrase; a pronoun is not (e.g. *please pass me that book* (determiner); *you can't do that* (pronoun)).
- Determiners that refer to quantity can be the hardest to spot.
- Always check through the use of all words that could be determiners.

GRAMMAR

 **Try this**

1 Tick ✔ the two sentences that use <u>these</u> as a **determiner**.

                                                                                            Tick **two**.

I have got some of <u>these</u>. ☐

Do you like <u>these</u> pictures? ☐

Are you looking for <u>these</u>? ☐

<u>These</u> games are my favourites. ☐

2 Add the correct **determiners** from the box to the passage below.

any   some   the

Jack wants to design _____ imaginary creatures, but he can't find _____ pencils in _____ box.

3 Add a correct **determiner** to each of the gaps in the passage below.

I would like to make _____ cakes but we don't have _____ eggs. I will try _____ recipe instead because it doesn't need them.

4 Underline all the **determiners** in the passage below.

This science experiment is quite difficult. It should take an hour but some children may need more time to complete it.

5 Add a suitable **determiner** to each gap in the passage below.

Archie found _____ book about ants in the cupboard, but it doesn't have _____ pictures so he would rather use _____ different one.

6 Tick ✔ all the sentences that contain a **determiner**.

Do you like this? ☐

Please pass those biscuits. ☐

Can I have this chair please? ☐

My favourite is this one. ☐

7 Circle the **determiners** in the sentences below.

A letter had arrived that morning. The family sat at the table waiting for it to be opened. Would it hold some surprises?

GRAMMAR

Subordinating and coordinating conjunctions

To achieve the higher score, you need to recognise and use the different **conjunctions**.

What you need to know

- **Conjunctions** join phrases and clauses.
- Conjunctions can be grouped into types, according to their function in a sentence.
- **Coordinating conjunctions** join two **main clauses** (e.g. *and*, *but*, *or*).
- **Subordinating conjunctions** join a main clause and a **subordinate clause** (e.g. *because*, *as*, *so*, *if*, *although*, *despite*, *unless*, *when*, *after*, *before*, *while*, *since*, *until*, *during*, *where*).
- Subordinating conjunctions can also be relative pronouns and introduce a relative clause (e.g. *who*, *which*, *where*, *when* and *that*). You need to be able to identify the function of words in a sentence.

Let's practise

Use two of the **conjunctions** in the box to correctly complete the sentence below.

| although | but | unless | when |

_____ you visit the zoo, make sure you go to the aquarium _____ you have a fear of confined spaces.

1 Read the question and read it again. What is it asking?

The question is asking you to use correct conjunctions to complete the sentence.

2 Read the sentence carefully so that you know what it means. Read the conjunctions and think about their purpose. Try the conjunctions where you think they will fit.

Although and *but* don't make sense if you use them in the sentence. So *when* and *unless* must be the correct conjunctions.

3 Check your answer.

<u>When</u> you visit the zoo, make sure you go to the aquarium <u>unless</u> you have a fear of confined spaces.

Top tip

- Conjunctions join clauses. Look for the two clauses, and find the word that joins them together.

GRAMMAR

 **Try this**

1 Circle all the **conjunctions** in the sentence below.

The magician told jokes while she did her tricks, but they were not very funny and the audience didn't laugh.

2 Add the most suitable **conjunction** from the box to the sentence below.

| unless   while   despite   or |

I can't help you _____ you tell me what you don't understand.

3 Write suitable **conjunctions** to complete the sentence below.

Charlie is good fun _____ he can be grumpy at times;

_____ he doesn't get his own way, he usually sulks.

4 Underline all the **conjunctions** in the passage below.

Unless we leave now, we will be caught in the rain and the picnic will be ruined. No one likes to eat soggy sandwiches outside when they could be warm indoors.

5 Tick ✔ one box in each row to show whether the underlined word is used as a **subordinating conjunction** or a **preposition**.

Sentence	Subordinating conjunction	Preposition
After we have been swimming, let's have a hot chocolate.		
Can you collect the newspaper after breakfast?		
Shall we have one last dive before we get out of the pool?		
Henry will be in Scotland until January.		
Jasmin can play with us until her sister comes to collect her.		

6 Complete the passage below using **subordinating conjunctions** from the box. Use each conjunction only once.

| because   even though   when |

Gemma was trying hard with her French homework _____ she found it difficult. She had missed the lesson _____ the class had learned the words to write about your family _____ she had been ill.

21

GRAMMAR

Main clauses and subordinate clauses

To achieve the higher score, you need to recognise and use **main** and **subordinate clauses**.

⭐ What you need to know

- Two main clauses are joined together by the conjunctions *and, or, but, so*.
- A subordinate clause on its own is not a complete sentence. It includes a subordinating conjunction (e.g. *because, as, so, if, although, despite, unless*).
- The subordinate clause can appear before, inside or after a main clause.
- A main clause makes sense on its own.
- **Watch out:** Some words can function as prepositions or as conjunctions, depending on their role in the sentence (*before, since, after*). A preposition introduces only a noun phrase (e.g. *before the show*) in a sentence. A subordinating conjunction introduces a whole clause, which includes a verb (e.g. *before we watched the show*) in a sentence.

⭐ Let's practise

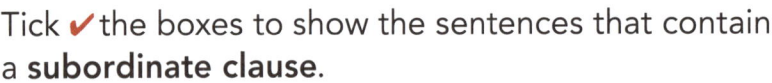

Tick ✔ the boxes to show the sentences that contain a **subordinate clause**.

We have been best friends since we first met. ☐
John has lived here since January. ☐
Since Alisha won the dance competition, she has practised even harder. ☐

1 Read the question and read it again. What is it asking?

The question is asking you to identify which sentences contain a subordinate clause.

2 Find the main clause in each sentence by checking which part of the sentence can work independently.

We have been best friends / John has lived here since January / She has practised even harder are all main clauses.

3 Check that the other parts of the sentence are subordinate clauses by finding the conjunction.

Since we first met / Since Alisha won the dance competition.

4 Check that the other use of *since* is not a conjunction.

In the second sentence *since* is not a conjunction because it is followed only by a noun, not a verb.

5 Check your answer.

We have been best friends since we first met. ✔
Since Alisha won the dance competition, she has practised even harder. ✔

22

GRAMMAR

 **Try this**

1 Underline the **subordinate clauses** in the passage below.

Otters are an endangered species that require very clean water in which to live. They have increased in number in some parts of England since rivers have become less polluted.

2 Add the correct words to complete the **subordinate clauses**.

| that   although   unless   when |

The school play will be a great success _____ Sam forgets his lines again. _____ he has spent ages learning them, _____ he goes on stage, he sometimes gets so nervous _____ he forgets them.

3 Complete the sentence below with a **subordinate clause**.

Please feed the cat before _____.

4 Underline the **main clause** in the sentence below.

My favourite cousin, who lives in Germany, is coming to visit.

5 Tick ✔ the sentences in which the underlined words form a **subordinate clause**.

Bats generally fly after dark. ☐

Birds puff up their feathers when the weather is very cold. ☐

Because they have incredible night vision, owls can hunt at night. ☐

If you feed the birds in your garden, they will visit you regularly. ☐

Top tips

- Do the clauses make a complete sentence on their own? If so, they are main clauses. If not, they are subordinate clauses.
- A subordinate clause begins with a subordinating conjunction such as *while, if, when, because* (see page 20).

GRAMMAR

Relative clauses

To achieve the higher score, you need to recognise and use **relative clauses**.

What you need to know

- A relative clause adds extra information about a noun or noun phrase. The sentence makes sense without it.
- A relative clause contains a verb (because it is a clause).
- It often begins with a relative pronoun: *who, which, when, where* or *that*. The relative pronoun may be omitted in some cases: *Paul, [who is] a great cook, made my birthday cake.*
- A relative clause is a type of subordinate clause.

Let's practise

Circle the **relative clause** in the sentence below.
The horse that is looking over the fence belongs to Aidan.

 Read the question and read it again. What is it asking? | The question is asking you to identify the relative clause.

 Find the nouns in the sentence. | *horse, fence* and *Aidan* are nouns.

 Check if the nouns are followed by a clause beginning with *who, which, when, where* or *that*. | The noun *horse* is followed by *that*. So *that* is the beginning of the relative clause.

 Find the end of the clause. Identify all the words that relate to the horse. | *that is looking over the fence* tells you about the horse, and so does *belongs to Aidan*.

 Check that the sentence makes sense if you remove the relative clause. | *The horse* is not a sentence. *The horse belongs to Aidan* makes sense as a sentence. So, *that is looking over the fence* is the relative clause.

 Check that you have circled the relative clause. | The horse ⟨that is looking over the fence⟩ belongs to Aidan.

GRAMMAR

 **Try this**

1 Circle the **relative clause** in the sentence below.

Rob's sister who lives in Canada is coming to visit next week.

2 Tick ✔ the sentences below in which <u>that</u> is used to begin a **relative clause**.

I can't understand <u>that</u> question. ☐

The wind blasted through the door <u>that</u> Kate had left open. ☐

The trees <u>that</u> Tom planted last year were growing well. ☐

At the end of <u>that</u> street, you will find a post box for your letter. ☐

3 Rewrite the sentence below adding a **relative clause**. Remember to punctuate your answer correctly.

I have moved the books.

_____

4 Add the correct **relative pronouns** from the box to the sentences below.

| when   where   which |

Our class went to see a dinosaur skeleton _____ is thousands of years old. It was found _____ builders were digging a site for the new museum _____ the skeleton is now displayed.

5 Which sentence contains a **relative clause**?

Tick **one**.

My Mum said that I could go to the cinema. ☐

Although I was late, I didn't miss anything. ☐

The girl who lives on my Gran's street is in my class. ☐

We are visiting the library next Tuesday. ☐

Top tip

- *That* is not always a relative pronoun. It can be a determiner (see page 18). For example, I like *that* picture. To check whether it begins a relative clause, check if it is followed by a verb (e.g. I like the picture *that is hanging in the hall*.).

GRAMMAR

Noun phrases

To achieve the higher score, you need to recognise and use **noun phrases**.

What you need to know

- A noun phrase includes the noun and any adjectives to describe it. A noun phrase gives detail to a noun. The determiner is part of the noun phrase.
- Information about the noun can appear in front of or after the noun, or in both places.
- A noun phrase can contain more than nouns, adjectives and determiners. *The very small creature in the box* is a noun phrase, and it contains an adverb (*very*) and a prepositional phrase (*in the box*). All the 'extra' words tell us more about the noun *creature*.

Let's practise

Underline all the **noun phrases** in the sentence below.
My annoying little brother is constantly playing with his noisy new electronic game.

1	Read the question and read it again. What is it asking?	The question is asking you to find all the noun phrases.
2	Find the nouns.	*Brother* and *game* are the nouns.
3	Find the words which add information about *brother*. Don't forget the determiner.	*My annoying little* refers to *brother*. *My* is the determiner.
4	Find the words which add information about *game*.	*His noisy new electronic* refers to *game*.
5	Underline the noun phrases. Check your answer.	<u>My annoying little brother</u> is constantly playing with <u>his noisy new electronic game</u>.

Try this

1 Underline the longest possible **noun phrase** in the sentence below.

   The oak tree at the end of the garden is great for climbing.

2 Rewrite the sentence below to expand the **noun phrase**. Remember to punctuate your answer correctly.

   Susie is proud of her basketball skills. _____

3 Circle all the **noun phrases** in the sentence below.

   The evening wind blew through the creaking trees and made a ghostly noise.

GRAMMAR

Subject and object

To achieve the higher score, you need to identify the **subject** and **object** of sentences.

⭐ What you need to know

- All sentences contain a **subject**. This tells you *who* or *what* <u>does</u> the action.
- Some sentences contain an **object**. The object is *who* or *what* the action <u>is done to</u>.
- There can be more than one subject and more than one object in a sentence.

⭐ Let's practise

Write **S** (**subject**) or **O** (**object**) in each of the boxes in the sentence below.

We threw the crusts of our sandwiches to the ducks and
☐   ☐   ☐

they quickly swallowed the pieces.
☐   ☐

1 Read the question and read it again. What is it asking?

The question is asking you to find the subjects and the objects.

2 Find the verbs.

Threw and swallowed are the verbs.

3 Find the subjects by asking yourself who (or what) is doing the action.

We threw so we is the subject and they swallowed so they is the subject. Write S in the boxes below We and they.

4 Find the objects by asking who or what the verbs are happening to.

Crusts are what is thrown, ducks are what they are thrown to and pieces are what is swallowed. Write O in the box below these words.

5 Check that you have written *S* and *O* in the correct boxes.

We threw the crusts of our sandwiches to the ducks and
  S   O   O

they quickly swallowed the pieces.
  S   O

✏️ Try this

1 Circle the **objects** and underline the **subjects** in the sentences below.

Joshua plays the guitar very well.

Yuri makes breakfast for his sister.

We are visiting our cousin's house.

27

GRAMMAR

Subject and verb agreement

To achieve the higher score, you need to make the **subject** and **verb** of a sentence agree.

⭐ What you need to know

- In the **present tense**, regular verbs change according to how many people are doing them (e.g. I *am eating* dinner. We *are eating* dinner.).
- To be correct, you must know the difference between singular and plural subjects. Look out for nouns that refer to a set of things (e.g. a bunch, a class, a collection). A bunch contains more than one flower but it refers to one bunch so it is singular. So *That bunch of flowers is beautiful,* not *That bunch of flowers are beautiful.*

⭐ Let's practise

Write the correct form of the **verb** in the gap.

to have

A pod of whales _____ been sighted close to our coast.

1	Read the question and read it again. What is it asking?	The question is asking you to choose the correct verb form to agree with the subject.
2	Find the subject. Is it singular or plural?	The subject is *A pod of whales. Pod* is singular.
3	Is the verb singular or plural?	There is just one pod so the verb is singular.
4	Check you have written the correct answer.	to have A pod of whales **has** been sighted close to our coast.

⭐ Top tip

- Focus on the first part of the noun phrase, e.g. <u>herd</u> of goats, <u>collections</u> of pictures to know whether to use a plural or singular verb form.

GRAMMAR

1 Circle the **correct words** for the sentence below.

The army **are**/**is** helping with today's event. The soldiers **are**/**is** ready to help you all to find your way.

2 Circle the **correct words** to complete the sentences below.

The school **are**/**is** holding a competition.

The teachers **are**/**is** giving an assembly.

Each team of pupils **are**/**is** trying hard to win the competition.

A bunch of flowers **are**/**is** given to thank the volunteers.

3 Tick ✔ the **sentences** below that are correct.

Most pupils are keen to help with the concert. ☐

Both girls and boys wants to be scientists. ☐

The library is closed. ☐

A litter of puppies have been born today. ☐

4 Rewrite the sentence below to make the **subject** and **verb** agree. Remember to punctuate your answer correctly.

David buy a book.

_____

5 Explain what is **incorrect** about the sentence below.

My cousin come home tomorrow.

_____

6 Circle the correct **verb form** to complete the sentences below.

In the park, there **was**/**were** plenty of ducks to feed.

The children **was**/**were** in the library waiting for the artist.

The last time I saw Baljit and Jackie **was**/**were** at the station.

29

GRAMMAR

Verbs in the progressive and perfect tenses

To achieve the higher score, you need to recognise the **present** and **past progressive tenses** and the **present** and **past perfect tenses** and be able to construct these verb forms.

What you need to know

- Progressive forms refer to an action that is continuous, e.g. I *am reading* this book at the moment.
- Progressive forms are made of two parts:
  - the verb *to be* + a verb ending in *-ing*.
  - **Present progressive** = I *am running*, He *is thinking*.
  - **Past progressive** = I *was reading*, You *were writing*, He, she or it *was watching*.
- Perfect forms have two parts. The **present perfect** tense refers to an action that begins in the past and continues to the present (e.g. *We have lived here for five years.*). The **past perfect** tense shows that one action has happened before another when both are in the past (e.g. *I had seen you before you saw me.*).
- Progressive and perfect **verb forms** are made with two verbs – an **auxiliary verb** and a main verb (e.g. progressive = *was walking* and perfect = *have eaten*).

Let's practise

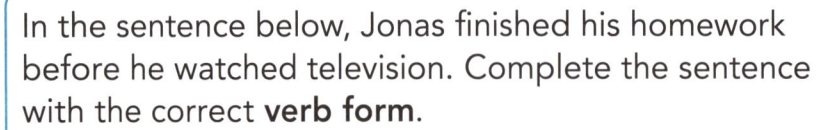

In the sentence below, Jonas finished his homework before he watched television. Complete the sentence with the correct **verb form**.

After Jonas _____ finished his homework, he watched his favourite television programme.

1	Read the question and read it again. What is it asking?	The question is asking you to choose the correct verb form.
2	Look for clues in the sentence that show you when the actions are happening.	*After* indicates that there is a sequence of actions. Both actions are using past tense verb forms.
3	Try the possible options for the gap: *was, has, had*.	Past perfect is correct so add the additional part of the verb: *had*.
4	Check your answer.	After Jonas __had__ finished his homework, he watched his favourite television programme.

30

GRAMMAR

 **Try this**

1 Tick ✔ one box in each row to show which sentences below are written using the **progressive verb form** and which are using the **perfect verb form**.

Sentence	Present progressive	Present perfect
Daniel is making dinner this evening.		
Lucy has made drinks for all the party guests.		
The children are lining up for lunch.		
We had arrived on time but the others were late.		

2 Underline all the verbs in the sentence below in the **past progressive** tense.

In the morning, we couldn't go out because it was raining, but then the weather changed and the sun was shining in the afternoon.

3 Add a **present perfect verb form** to complete the sentence below.

Sam _____ in this house since he was born.

4 Rewrite the sentence below using the **present perfect form** of the verb. Remember to punctuate your answer correctly.

The twins learn to play dominoes today.

_____

5 Write the verb in the gap in the **past perfect verb form**.

When Jack's parents got up, they saw that he _____ breakfast for them.

Top tip

- Perfect and progressive tenses are made of two verbs (e.g. *have/had* learned or *is/was* learning).

31

GRAMMAR

Passive and active voices

To achieve the higher score, you need to recognise the **active** and **passive voices**.

⭐ What you need to know

- Most sentences are written in the **active voice** (e.g. *George broke the window*).
  They follow a subject + verb + object order (see page 27).
- Sometimes, a different word order is used: object + verb + subject
  (e.g. *The window was broken by George* or *The window was broken.*).
  This is called the **passive voice**.
- The passive voice is used when:
  - the writer wants to focus on the object (e.g. *the window*);
  - the writer doesn't want to tell who did the action (e.g. *George*);
  - the person is unknown (e.g. *A vase was mysteriously broken.*);
  - it doesn't matter who did it (e.g. *The test tube was placed on the Bunsen burner.*).

⭐ Let's practise

Rewrite the sentence below using the **passive voice**.
Josh switched on the lights.

1	Read the question and read it again. What is it asking?	The question is asking you to rewrite the sentence using the passive voice.
2	Find the subject and the object in the sentence.	*Josh* is the subject. *Lights* is the object.
3	Swap the order of the subject and object so that the object is first.	The lights / switched on / Josh.
4	Now, change the verb to make the sentence make sense.	**The lights were switched on by Josh.**
5	Check your answer.	

32

GRAMMAR

 *Try this*

1 Tick ✔ one box in each row of the table to show whether each sentence is in the **passive** or the **active voice**.

Sentence	Passive	Active
Last night, trees were knocked over by the wind.		
My brother loves watching cowboy films.		
My boots were chewed by our dogs.		
Oscar designed a super castle.		

2 Rewrite the sentence below in the **passive voice**. Remember to punctuate your answer correctly.

Our school won the football match.

_____

3 Rewrite the sentence below in the **active voice**. Remember to punctuate your answer correctly.

The cake was eaten by the children.

_____

4 Tick ✔ one box in each row of the table to show whether each sentence is in the **passive** or the **active voice**.

Sentence	Passive	Active
The whales were feeding on a school of fish.		
The fish had been trapped in a net.		
The boats were followed by dolphins.		
Dolphins are sometimes caught in fishing nets.		

5 Explain why the **passive voice** has been used in this sentence.

The test tube was warmed over a flame.

_____

GRAMMAR

Subjunctive verb forms

To achieve the higher score, you need to recognise verbs in the subjunctive form.

What you need to know

- The **subjunctive verb form** can be used when the speaker suggests or recommends something and wants to sound formal.
- The subjunctive can be used in sentences that suggest or recommend:
  - *I suggest that, He recommends that, She advises that, We insist that*
- Popular uses of the subjunctive are in the sentences beginning *If I were you …* or *I wish I were ….*
- The subjunctive very often uses the verb *to be* in an unusual way.

Let's practise

Tick ✔ the sentence below that is in the **subjunctive** form.

Tick **one**.

He wishes he were on holiday. ☐
She remembered to phone her aunt. ☐
I was happy because it was my birthday. ☐

1	Read the question and read it again. What is it asking?	The question is asking you to find the sentence in the subjunctive form.
2	Check for the popular forms, *If (I) were you* or *(I) wish (I) were*.	The first sentence includes *He wishes he were*.
3	Check that there is not another possible answer. Check that all the other verbs agree in the normal way.	*She remembered*, *I was* are both used in the normal way.
4	Tick the box to show the sentence in the subjunctive form.	He wishes he were on holiday. ✔
5	Check your answer.	

34

GRAMMAR

 **Try this**

1 Circle the **subjunctive** form to complete the sentence below.

Olivia recommended that Sam **join** / **joins** the school cricket team.

2 Underline the verb in the **subjunctive** form in the sentence below.

Jack suggested that his brother make the wedding speech as he was too nervous.

3 Tick ✔ the boxes to show which sentences are written using the **subjunctive** form.

If I were you, I would practise my guitar a little more often. ☐

If you look behind the curtains, you will find where Archie is hiding. ☐

If you recommend that he study harder, he will do it. ☐

If I go on holiday, I will bring a present back for you. ☐

4 Complete this sentence using the **subjunctive** form. Choose one verb from the box below.

| am is was were |

If I _____ you, I would not be quite so rude.

5 Rewrite the verb underlined in the sentence below so that it uses the **subjunctive** form.

The doctor recommends that Anna <u>eats</u> more fruit each day to stay healthy.

_____

6 Tick ✔ the boxes to show which sentences are written in the **subjunctive** form.

She was ready to leave on time. ☐

I wish Ben were here as he would know what to do. ☐

Lola insisted that her sister help with the washing up. ☐

Max asked if he could borrow my bike. ☐

35

GRAMMAR

Standard English and formality

To achieve the higher score, you need to know how to identify and use **Standard English**, and to identify differences between informal and formal language.

What you need to know

- Standard English is the form of the English language widely accepted as the usual correct form. It includes both vocabulary and sentence structures.
- People may use other expressions in speaking or informal writing, but Standard English is used for formal communication.
- You will need to be aware of non-Standard English variations that may be frequently used in your region of the country.

Let's practise

Rewrite the underlined word in the sentence below using **Standard English**.

Hayley is the player <u>what</u> scored the final goal.

1 Read the question and read it again. What is it asking?

The question is asking you to rewrite non-Standard use of a word, using Standard English.

2 Read the sentence in your head and try out other options that could replace 'what'.

Who or *that* could replace *what*.

3 Check that your ideas work grammatically.

Who and *that* are both relative pronouns so either one would be correct. Write one of these options on the line.
Hayley is the player <u>who / that</u> scored the final goal.

36

GRAMMAR

Try this

1 Rewrite the sentence below changing the underlined words to **Standard English**. Remember to punctuate your answer correctly.

Ed <u>ain't</u> got <u>no</u> more money left.

_____

2 Match the underlined words in the sentences with their more **formal** options.

Could you <u>find out</u> who spilled the paint?	endeavour
You should <u>attempt</u> to solve each problem.	accompany
We shall <u>go to</u> the prize-giving on Monday.	ascertain
Would you like to <u>come with</u> me to the theatre?	attend

3 Rewrite the sentence below using **Standard English**. Remember to punctuate your answer correctly.

Alex done less lengths of the pool than me.

_____

4 Tick ✔ one box in each row to show whether the word <u>fewer</u> or <u>less</u> should be added to each sentence.

Sentence	Add <u>fewer</u>	Add <u>less</u>
Rhinos are in danger of extinction as there are far _____ breeding pairs alive now.		
Racehorses are fast but can increase their speed much _____ quickly than a cheetah.		
Research has found that _____ people are taking regular exercise than once was the norm.		
Because they are larger, you'll need _____ strawberries than raspberries in your recipe.		

Top tip

- Some questions may ask you to tick/circle the most formal sentence/option. For these questions, you will need to look at the language used and imagine they are on a scale of formality (from formal to informal). Then you can identify which one is most formal.

PUNCTUATION

Capital letters, full stops, exclamation marks and question marks

To achieve the higher score, you need to use **capital letters**, **full stops**, **exclamation marks** and **question marks** in the right places in sentences.

What you need to know

- Every sentence begins with a **capital letter** and ends with either a **full stop**, an **exclamation mark** for **exclamations** or a **question mark** for questions.
- Proper nouns require a capital letter (e.g. for names of places, people, nationalities, days and months, brand names).

Let's practise

> Add the correct **capital letters** and **full stops** to the passage below.
>
> arthur took his dogs, henry and hettie, on holiday to wales they had a super time even though it was very cold in february

1 Read the question and read it again. What is it asking?

The question is asking you to find beginnings and endings of sentences, and where to use capital letters for proper nouns.

2 Read the passage carefully to help you find the sentence ending(s). Mark where each full stop should go. Don't forget the final one.

arthur took his dogs, henry and hettie, on holiday to wales**.** they had a super time even though it was very cold in february**.**

3 Check whether there are any names of people, places or brands in the sentence that would need a capital letter.

Arthur, **H**enry, **H**ettie, **W**ales, and **F**ebruary

4 Check for any beginnings of sentences. Add a capital letter.

Arthur took his dogs, **H**enry and **H**ettie, on holiday to **W**ales. **T**hey had a super time even though it was very cold in **F**ebruary.

5 Check your answer.

PUNCTUATION

Try this

1 Add a **punctuation mark** from the box to each sentence below. You may use each one only once.

> ? ! .

How interesting that was ___

What would you like to do ___

Although you're late, it's great to see you ___

2 Add **capital letters** and **full stops** to the passage below.

the door opened suddenly and the class all turned to look the special guest had arrived everyone had been looking forward to this moment

3 Rewrite the sentence below adding correct **capital letters** and **punctuation**.

at heathton school, our classes learn spanish and french

_____

Select one of the words that has a capital letter and explain why a **capital letter** is used.

_____

4 Why does the sentence below have an **exclamation mark**?

What a dreadful thing to say!

_____

5 Add **capital letters**, **full stops** and a **question mark** to the passage below.

I had never seen such a strange creature whatever could it be living in spain was turning out to be full of surprises

6 Underline the words that need **capital letters** in the sentence below.

We will visit london next tuesday and see 10 downing street, the home of the prime minister.

Top tip

- Remember that all parts of proper nouns need capital letters (e.g. *Sally Smith*, *United Kingdom*, *Rising Stars Limited*).

PUNCTUATION

Commas

To achieve the higher score, you need to use **commas** to mark clauses or phrases, to separate items in a list and to clarify meanings.

What you need to know

- Commas are used to separate items in a list and to mark phrases or clauses.
- The use of a comma can change the meaning of a sentence.
- A comma splice is a common comma error, when a comma is used incorrectly instead of a full stop or **semi-colon**.

Let's practise

Add **commas** in the correct places to the sentence below.
Before we go on the bike ride check your tyres brakes and lights.

1. Read the question and read it again. What is it asking? — The question is asking you to show where commas should go.

2. Read the sentence clearly to find where the clauses meet. — There are two parts to this sentence and the clauses meet after *ride*. Add a comma.

3. Check if there is a list in the sentence. — *Tyres brakes and lights* is a list.

4. Separate these items with commas, remembering that there is no comma before *and*. — Check your tyres, brakes and lights.

5. Check your answer. — Before we go on the bike ride, check your tyres, brakes and lights.

Top tips

- Remember to use two commas to mark an embedded clause or phrase (e.g. *Oscar, my favourite cat, often sits on my shoulder.*).
- Look out for adverbial phrases and clauses that require a comma (e.g. *Suddenly, I saw it. Next, it saw me.*).

PUNCTUATION

Try this

1 Add the necessary **commas** to the sentence below.

Although Alma loves hamsters mice and rats she doesn't like gerbils.

2 Rewrite the sentence below using **commas** correctly.

Quickly before it rains run inside.

_____

3 Add **commas** to clarify the meaning of this sentence.

My favourite desserts are strawberry and vanilla ice-cream apple pie with custard and fresh fruit salad.

4 Add a **comma** to change the meaning of the sentence below.

I will tell Jake.

5 Explain how a **comma** changes the meaning of the sentence below.

Can you help Susie?
Can you help, Susie?

_____

6 Add the correct **commas** to the sentence below.

I play tennis which is my favourite sport at the weekends.

7 Tick ✔ the boxes to show the sentences in which **commas** are used correctly.

Two cars, a red one and a green one, were racing side by side. ☐

A country, with a tropical climate, can be extremely hot. ☐

A flock, of geese, spend the winter on a lake nearby. ☐

Trains, especially high-speed ones, are a comfortable way to travel. ☐

PUNCTUATION

Inverted commas

To achieve the higher score, you need to use **inverted commas** to show direct speech.

What you need to know

- **Inverted commas** are sometimes called **speech marks**.
- Inverted commas are put around what the speaker says, e.g.
    Daisy said, "I love swimming."
    "I love swimming," said Daisy.
    "I love swimming," said Daisy, "and diving."
- A new speech sentence starts with a capital letter, even if unspoken words introduce what the speaker says, e.g.
    Daisy asked, "Would anyone like to go swimming?"
- The reporting clause that identifies who spoke (*said Daisy* or *Daisy said*) should be separated from what is spoken with a comma.
- The spoken sentence could end with a question mark or exclamation mark, instead of a full stop.
- **Punctuation** linked to speech always goes inside the speech marks.

Let's practise

Add the correct **inverted commas** and **commas** to the sentence below.

Can we go to the park asked Ella or even to the beach?

1 Read the question and read it again. What is it asking?

The question is asking you to add inverted commas and commas to a sentence.

2 Identify which words are spoken.

Can we go to the park and *or even to the beach?* are the words being spoken.

3 The words *asked Ella* identify who spoke. Separate this clause from the rest of the sentence using commas.

Can we go to the park**,** asked Ella**,** or even to the beach?

4 Place the inverted commas around what the speaker says.

"Can we go to the park**,"** asked Ella**, "**or even to the beach?**"**

5 Check your answer.

42

PUNCTUATION

Try this

1 Which sentence uses **inverted commas** correctly?

Tick **one**.

"Mrs Archer asked, Which city is the capital of France?" ☐

Mrs Archer asked, "Which city is the capital of France?" ☐

Mrs Archer asked. "Which city is the capital of France?" ☐

Mrs Archer asked, "Which city is the capital of France"? ☐

2 Add correct **inverted commas** to the sentence below.

Please sit down here requested the dentist.

3 Add correctly placed **commas** and **full stops** to each of the sentences below.

" My brother is a champion chess player " boasted Archie

Lucia replied " My sister wins competitions too "

4 Add correct **punctuation** to the sentence below.

We won the match shouted the team excitedly

5 Rewrite the sentence below as direct speech. Remember to punctuate your answer correctly.

Freddie asked Joe if he knew how to play chess.

Freddie asked Joe, _____

6 Rewrite the sentence below using correct **punctuation** for direct speech.

I will tidy my room promised Jake after I finish this game.

_____

Top tip

- If you place the commas first, it is easier to make sure they are placed correctly inside or outside the inverted commas.

PUNCTUATION

Apostrophes

To achieve the higher score, you need to use **apostrophes** correctly.

⭐ What you need to know

- When something belongs to plural persons or things, add the **apostrophe** after the last letter of the owners: *the foxes' hole*.
- Nouns that refer to a group need a final *s* to show possession. Then, place the apostrophe before that *s* (e.g. *children's*, *herd's*, *people's*).
- Apostrophes are used in two different ways:
  - omission – when letters are missed out of a word (**contraction**).
  - possession – to show belonging / ownership.

⭐ Let's practise

Rewrite the sentence below using a **contraction**.
You should not shout here.

1	Read the question and read it again. What is it asking?	The question is asking you to find words that can be contracted.
2	First, check to find the words that can be contracted.	*should not*
3	Write the contraction using an apostrophe to mark the missing letter.	*shouldn't* You **shouldn't** shout here.
4	Check your answer.	

⭐ Top tips

- Beware of words that join together or change when the apostrophe is added, (e.g. *could not = couldn't*; *will not = won't*).
- **Watch out:** *Its* and *it's* are often confused. *It's* is *it is*, shortened. *Its* is used for possession. There is no apostrophe in *its*, for possession.
- **Watch out:** Apostrophes of possession can be tricky with plurals (e.g. *Foxes' tails are bushy* but *The fox's tail was injured.*).

PUNCTUATION

Try this

1 Change the examples below to include a **possessive apostrophe**.

Example: *the bag that belongs to Kim = Kim's bag*

   a) the mast belonging to the boat
   _____

   b) the hats belonging to the sailors
   _____

   c) the source of the river
   _____

   d) the mouths of the rivers
   _____

   e) sunshine of today
   _____

   f) rain of last week
   _____

2 Write the words below as **contractions**.

   he would not   _____

   she will   _____

   you must not   _____

3 Rewrite the words that should have **apostrophes** in the sentence below.

I didnt think itd be possible to climb the cliff because they hadnt brought their ropes.

_____   _____   _____

4 Rewrite the sentence below using correct **apostrophes** where necessary.

Theyve reached the mountains peak and planted the groups flag on the very top.

_____

5 Explain why **apostrophes** have been used for the words in the sentence below.

The pupils' books weren't in the cupboard.

pupils'   _____

weren't   _____

45

PUNCTUATION

Parenthesis

To achieve the higher score, you need to recognise the correct use of a **parenthesis**.

What you need to know

- A **parenthesis** is an extra part of the sentence. The sentence can make sense without it. There are three forms of punctuating parenthesis: commas, brackets and **dashes**. Writers choose which suits their style and purpose.

Let's practise

Add two **dashes** to the sentence below.
The hairy mammoth though extinct for centuries never fails to interest children.

1 Read the question and read it again. What is it asking?

The question is asking you to identify the part of the sentence which could be in parenthesis between dashes.

2 Find the extra information in the sentence.

Though extinct for centuries is extra information about *The hairy mammoth*. This can be placed between dashes.

3 Check your answer.

The hairy mammoth – though extinct for centuries – never fails to interest children.

Try this

1 Which of these sentences uses **dashes** correctly?

Tick **one**.

Jena always has – her favourite breakfast toast – and ice-cream on Sundays. ☐

Jena always has her favourite breakfast – toast and ice-cream – on Sundays. ☐

Jena – always has her favourite breakfast – toast and ice-cream on Sundays. ☐

Jena always has – her favourite – breakfast toast and ice-cream on Sundays. ☐

2 Rewrite the sentence below using brackets for **parenthesis**.

My sister much to my surprise gave me a present.

_____

3 Explain why **parenthesis** has been used in the sentence below.

On our trip to Australia – the home of my aunt – we saw kangaroos and kookaburras.

_____

PUNCTUATION

Colons, semi-colons, single dashes, hyphens and bullet points

To achieve the higher score, you need to recognise and use punctuation correctly.

What you need to know

- **Colons**, semi-colons and single dashes can all be used to mark the boundary between independent clauses. They make a link between two sentences with linked ideas. Colons can be used to introduce a list. Semi-colons can be used to separate items in a list.
- **Bullet points** are used to mark items in a list which is introduced by a colon.
- **Hyphens** are used to link two words together to make a compound noun.

Let's practise

Add a **semi-colon** to the passage below.
Ross didn't want to travel by plane he was afraid of flying.

1	Read the question and read it again. What is it asking?	The question is asking you to identify where a semi-colon should be used.
2	Find the sentences in the passage and put a pencil mark where you think they meet.	Ross didn't want to travel by plane / he was afraid of flying.
3	Check that each part of the sentence makes sense on its own. If they do, add the semi-colon.	Ross didn't want to travel by plane; he was afraid of flying.

Try this

1. Add a **semi-colon** to the sentence below.

   Whenever I see you, you make me smile you are my very best friend.

2. Rewrite the sentence below using a **dash**.

   It should not have happened in my opinion.

   _____

3. Rewrite the sentence below using a **colon** and **correct punctuation**.

   I eat a lot of fruit apples oranges plums

   _____

47

SPELLING

Prefixes and suffixes

To achieve the higher score, you need to add **prefixes** and **suffixes** to words.

★ What you need to know

- **Prefixes** are added at the beginning of a root word (see page 49) and **suffixes** at the end of a root word to make a new word.
- Prefixes usually change the meaning of a word (e.g. *agree – disagree*).
- Suffixes usually change a word's form (e.g. an adjective to a noun: *clever – cleverness*).

★ Let's practise

Circle the **prefix** from the box that can be added to both of the words below.

| dis- mis- re- un- | __introduce   __calculate |

1 Read the question and read it again. What is it asking?

The question is asking you to select the correct prefix that can be added to both words.

2 Try out each prefix with both words to find the one that makes sense.

disintroduce ✗ discalculate ✗. *Dis-* is not the answer. misintroduce ✗ miscalculate ✓. *Mis-* is not the answer. reintroduce ✓ recalculate ✓.

3 Check the other option to make sure.

unintroduce ✗ uncalculate ✗. *un-* is not correct so *re-* is the answer.

4 Circle your answer, then check it.

dis-   mis-   (re-)   un-

✏ Try this

1 Make new words by adding a correct **prefix** or **suffix** to these words.

Prefixes: **un- dis- re- sub-**   *Suffixes:* **-ness -ment -ful -ly**

conscious   standard   forgive   believe   judge   commence   thought

_____

2 Circle one **prefix** that can be added to both of these words.

dis- mis- un- pre-   __apprehend   __read

3 Underline the **suffixes** in the words below.

swiftest   fruitless   awareness   payment

SPELLING

Prefixes

To achieve the higher score, you need to correctly spell words with **prefixes**.

What you need to know

- Most prefixes are added to the beginning of root words without any changes in spelling. So, if a word begins with the same letter as the end of the prefix, both letters are used, e.g. *dis* + satisfy = di*ss*atisfy, *un* + necessary = u*nn*ecessary.
- Some prefixes have negative meanings: *dis* + appoint; *mis* + behave; *un* + do.
- Do not confuse *dis* and *des*:
  - When a word begins with dis, you can usually remove *dis* and a root word will still exist (e.g. *disappear* = *dis* + *appear*). When a word begins with *des*, it doesn't usually make sense if you remove the *des* (e.g. *despise*, *describe*).
- *in* means 'not' before words beginning with most letters, except:
  - before a root word starting with *l*, *in* becomes *il*;
  - before a root word starting with *m* or *p*, *in* becomes *im*;
  - before a root word starting with *r*, *in* becomes *ir*.

Try this

Use the rules above and the *Let's practise* flowchart on page 48 to help you answer the following questions.

1. Write the words below adding the correct **prefix**.

   capable   come   caution   social   similar   logical

   _____

2. Add the words to the table in the correct column, including the **prefix**.

   logical   measurable   advisable   plausible   relevant   perfection   regularity   legitimate

in-	im-	il-	ir-

3. Add one of the **prefixes** to each of the words below to make a new word. Some of the prefixes can be used more than once.

   anti- auto- inter- sub- super-

   a) city   _____
   b) biotic   _____
   c) normal   _____
   d) biography _____
   e) conscious _____
   f) natural   _____

Top tips

- Remember to keep the double letter if the prefix ends and the word begins with the same letter.
- Prefixes have different meanings:

  re = again or back   *sub* = under
  inter = between   *super* = above
  anti = against   *auto* = self

49

SPELLING

Suffixes: -tion, -ssion, -cian

To achieve the higher score, you need to correctly spell words containing these **suffixes**.

What you need to know

- The sound 'shun' at the end of words can be spelled in different ways.
  - *-tion* is the most common spelling of the 'shun' sound. It is used if the root word ends in *t* or *te* (e.g. invent = *invention*).
  - *-sion* is used if the word ends in *d* or *se* (e.g. revi<u>se</u> = *revision*, expan<u>d</u> = *expansion*).
  - *-cian* is used if the root word ends in *c* or *cs* (e.g. *music/musician*, *politics/politician*). These words often refer to a person's job.
  - *-ssion* is used if the root word ends in *ss* or *mit* (e.g. express = *expression*, permit = *permission*).

Try this

Use the rules above, the *Let's practise* flowchart on page 48 and your own knowledge to help you answer the following questions.

1. Underline the final letters of the root words, looking at the correct use of the **suffix**. Look, cover, say and write.

Root word	'shun' suffix	Look, cover, say and write
reject	rejection	
apprehend	apprehension	
calculate	calculation	

2. Name the jobs of the people who:

   work with electricity _____

   play music _____

   check your eyes _____

   work in politics _____

Top tip

- Remember to remove the final letter before the suffix, if necessary.

Suffixes: -ous, -tious, -cious

To achieve the higher score, you need to correctly spell words containing these **suffixes**.

What you need to know

- The suffixes *-ous*, *-tious* and *-cious* all make the sound 'shus'.
- Sometimes the root word is obvious (e.g. poison + *-ous* = *poisonous*).
- But sometimes there is no root word, so learn these common words: *enormous, fabulous, jealous, tremendous, obvious*.
- When adding suffixes to words ending with a vowel or *y*:
  - If the root ends in *e*, remove it before adding *ous*: fame = remove e = *famous*.
  - If the root ends in *y*, change it to *i* before adding *ous*:
    vary = y becomes i = *various*.
  - If there is an *ee* sound before the *ous* ending, it is usually spelled as *i* (e.g. *serious, obvious, curious*).
- A few words have *e* before *ous* (e.g. *hideous, spontaneous, courteous*).
- *-our* changes to *-or* before *-ous* is added (e.g. humour = humor = *humorous*).
- If the root word ends in *ce* the 'shus' sound is usually spelled as *-cious* (e.g. grace = *gracious*).
- If the root word ends in *-tion*, the 'shus' sound is usually spelled as *-tious* (e.g. ambition = *ambitious*). Exception: *anxious*.

Try this

Use the rules above and the *Let's practise* flowchart on page 48 to help you answer the following questions.

1 Add the **suffix** -ous to the words below:

mystery _____

study _____

glory _____

2 Add the correct **suffix** to these words ending in -ce.

grace _____

space _____

3 Organise these words into **three** groups according to the **suffixes**.

advantageous   cautious   hilarious   hideous   ambitious   delicious   courteous
simultaneous   curious   precious   infectious   devious

SPELLING

Suffixes: -able, -ably, -ible, -ibly

To achieve the higher score, you need to correctly spell words containing these **suffixes**.

What you need to know

- The *-able*/*-ably* ending is the most common spelling of this type of suffix.
- It is usually used when a complete root word can be heard before it (e.g. depend = *dependable*).
- It is also used with root words that can have the ending *-tion* (e.g. application = *applicable*).
- If the root word ends in *-ce* or *-ge*, the final *e* is kept (e.g. change = *changeable*). Exception: force = *forcible*.
- The *-ible* ending is often used when a complete root word can't be heard before it (e.g. *possible*/*possibly*). Exception: *sensible*.

Try this

Use the rules above and the *Let's practise* flowchart on page 48 to help you answer the following questions.

1 Look at the table and sort the words below into the correct columns.

adorably   applicable   unnoticeable   understandably   probably   reasonable
reachable   horrible   invisibly   accessible   irrevocable   comfortable   intelligible

Complete root word can be heard (-<u>able</u>/-<u>ably</u>)	No root word (-<u>ible</u>/-<u>ibly</u>)

2 Rewrite the words below, adding -<u>able</u> and -<u>ably</u>.

Root word	-<u>able</u>	-<u>ably</u>
pity		
avoid		
believe		
classify		

SPELLING

Suffixes: -ant, -ance, -ancy, -ent, -ence, -ency

To achieve the higher score, you need to correctly spell words containing these **suffixes**.

What you need to know

- A word with an -*ant* suffix spelling will also have an -*ance* and -*ancy* suffix if these forms of the word exist (e.g. important = *importance*).
- A word with an -*ent* suffix spelling will also have an -*ence* and -*ency* suffix if these forms of the word exist (e.g. evident = *evidence*).
- The -*ant*, -*ance*, -*ancy* suffixes are used after root words that can also have -*ation* endings (e.g. expect = expectation = *expectant*; toleration = *tolerance*).
- The -*ent*, -*ence*, -*ency* suffixes are used with words that have the following sounds:
  - soft c (e.g. *decency, innocence, licence, magnificent, complacent*);
  - soft g (e.g. *intelligence, urgent, emergency*);
  - qu (e.g. *frequency, sequence, consequence*).

Try this

Use the rules above and the *Let's practise* flowchart on page 48 to help you answer the following questions.

1 Read this short passage and find the -ent, -ence, or -ency words and the -ant, -ance, or -ancy words. Sort them into two groups.

> Blake stood before his audience. He had always enjoyed performance, but his experiences were in the classroom, not with this huge audience and he had a tendency to be nervous. However, Blake refused to allow the circumstances to shake his confidence. Momentarily, there was a disturbance at the back of the room, and he became hesitant. Then, he found his mental balance and began to demonstrate his competence in making balloon animals.

-ent, -ence, -ency words	-ant, -ance, -ancy words

2 Write the missing word endings.
   a) Your dog is very obedi_____.
   b) If you refuse to give up, you are being persist_____.

53

SPELLING

Words with *ei, eigh, ey, ay*

To achieve the higher score, you need to correctly spell words containing these combinations of letters.

What you need to know

- The long *ai* sound is spelled in a number of ways: *ei*, *eigh*, *ey* or *ay*. You must know which words use which groups of letters.

Try this

1 Complete the sentences with a word using the ei, eigh, ey or ay spelling.

   a) The person who lives next to me is my n_____.

   b) I love to ride on a s_____ in the snow.

Words with *ie, ei*

To achieve the higher score, you need to correctly spell words containing these combinations of letters.

What you need to know

- Many words are spelled with *ie* to make the long *ee* sound. However, there are exceptions: *friend*, *fierce*.
- The '*i* before *e* except after *c*' rule works for words where the sound after the *c* is a long *e* sound (e.g. *receive*, *deceive*). However, there are other words where the *ei* spelling does not say the long *ee* sound (e.g. *either*, *neither*, *leisure*, *their*, *weird*).

Try this

1 Add ie or ei to the words below.

   a) w____rd

   b) for____gn

   c) sover____gn

   d) forf____t

   e) retr____val

   f) obed____nce

SPELLING

Words with *ough*

To achieve the higher score, you need to correctly spell words containing this combination of letters.

★ What you need to know

- The *ough* spelling is used for many different sounds:

Sound	or	uff	long o (owe)	oo	off	short *u*	ow
Example	bought	tough	though	through	cough	thorough	plough

★ Let's practise

Add the correct *ough* word to complete the sentence.

Scientists have made a break_____ discovery.

1	Read the question and read it again. What is it asking?	The question is asking you to add an *ough* word in the gap to make a new word.
2	What complete word would make sense in the sentence?	The complete word could be break<u>through</u>.
3	Try a word with the 'ough' sound that would make sense in the gap.	The *ough* word must be *through*.
4	Check the sentence makes sense and the spelling of the new word is correct.	Scientists have made a break<u>through</u> discovery.

✏ Try this

1 Add the correct <u>ough</u> word to complete each sentence.

a) You o_____ to eat fruit each day.

b) This is the t_____ task I have ever been given.

2 Explain what each of these words means.

borough _____

bough _____

doughnut _____

drought _____

55

SPELLING

Word endings: *al, el, il, le*

To achieve the higher score, you need to correctly spell words that end with these letters.

What you need to know

- The *le* spelling is the most common spelling for the sound /e+l/ at the end of words. Nearly three quarters of words with this sound are spelled with *le*: *table, apple, bottle, little, middle, style*.
- Not many nouns end in *al* (but many adjectives do). Learn the commonly used nouns: *metal, pedal, capital, hospital, animal*.
- Adjectives: *accidental, alphabetical, additional, chemical, colossal, final, national*.
- The *el* spelling is used after word beginnings that end with *m, n, r, v, w* and often after *s*: *camel, tunnel, squirrel, travel, towel, tinsel*.

Let's practise

Complete each word with the <u>le</u> or <u>el</u> spelling.

edib_____   marv_____

1. Read the question and read it again. What is it asking?

   The question is asking you to make two new words with *el* or *le* endings.

2. Remind yourself which letters tell you when to use *el*: *m, n, r, v, w* and *s*.
   Then try the *le* and *el* endings for the words.

   edib**el** ✗   marv**el** ✓
   edib**le** ✓   marv**le** ✗

3. Check the spellings of your answers.

   edib**le**   marv**el**

Try this

1. Decide whether the word beginnings below will use the <u>le</u> or <u>el</u> spelling.

   a) mudd_____   d) flann_____   g) kenn_____

   b) pumm_____   e) incredib_____ h) arab_____

   c) icic_____   f) sprink_____   i) carous_____

2. Add *al* to these words to make them adjectives.

   a) classic_____   c) education_____   e) profession_____

   b) function_____ d) archaeologic_____ f) medic_____

SPELLING

Silent letters

To achieve the higher score, you need to correctly spell words containing **silent letters**.

⭐ What you need to know

- **Silent letters** appear in the spelling of a word, but are not heard when the words are spoken.

⭐ Let's practise

Circle the **silent letter** in each word below.
guilty   biscuit   hymn

1 Read the question and read it again. What is it asking?

The question is asking you to find the letter that is silent in each word.

2 Read each word. Which letters can be heard?

g u i l t y   b i s c u i t   h y m n

3 Check you have circled the silent letters.

g(u)ilty   bis(c)uit   hym(n)

✏️ Try this

1 Sort the words below according to which letter is **silent**.

anchor   doubt   solemn   wrist   knell   tomb   psychology   glisten   Wednesday
wretch   knead   receipt   knuckle   stomach   debt   hustle   guitar   chrome   sword

2 Many words for parts of the body have **silent letters**. Write the words. Circle the silent letters.

a) _____ d) _____
b) _____ e) _____
c) _____ f) _____

3 Underline the words with **silent letters** in the passage below.

On Wednesday, I went to the toy shop to buy a sword. I asked for a receipt so that there could be no doubt I had paid for it. The chrome glistened in the sunlight when I held it up, but it was quite heavy so it made my wrist ache a bit.

57

SPELLING

Homophones

To achieve the higher score, you need to correctly spell a variety of **homophones**.

What you need to know

- **Homophones** are words that sound the same but have different meanings.
- You need to know these frequently used homophones: *there*, *their* and *they're*; *to*, *too* and *two*; *your* and *you're*; *whose* and *who's*.

Let's practise

Add the correct spelling of the word in the sentences.

baron / barren

A desert is a b_____ place.
The b_____ supports the king.

1 Read the question and read it again. What is it asking?

The question is asking you to choose one of the words that make sense in each sentence.

2 What does each word mean?

barren means empty
a baron is someone of noble birth

3 Try each word in each sentence. Which sentences make sense?

A desert is a <u>baron</u> place. ✗
The <u>barren</u> supports the king. ✗
A desert is a <u>barren</u> place. ✔
The <u>baron</u> supports the king. ✔

4 Check your answer.

A desert is a <u>barren</u> place.
The <u>baron</u> supports the king.

Try this

1 Add the correct word from the box to each sentence.

| stationary / stationery | coarse / course | accept / except | affect / effect |

a) When a car is parked, it is s_____.

b) You write a letter on s_____.

c) Make sure you run on the correct c_____.

d) This cloth is rough and c_____.

e) Please _____cept this token of my appreciation.

f) You can do anything you like _____cept jump on the beds.

g) If you do not sleep, it will _____ffect your concentration.

h) Reading a story has a calming _____ffect on a lively class.

SPELLING

Synonyms and antonyms

To achieve the higher score, you need to know the terms **synonym** and **antonym**, and identify examples.

★ What you need to know

- **Synonyms** are words that have the same meaning.
- **Antonyms** are words that have opposite meanings.

★ Let's practise

Tick ✔ the words that are the **antonyms** of victory.

triumph, success ☐   hesitation, pause ☐
defeat, loss ☐   popularity, fame ☐

1	Read the question and read it again. What is it asking?	The question is asking you to find words which mean the opposite (antonym) of *victory*.
2	Try out each pair of words to find the opposite of *victory*.	*Triumph* and *success* can mean the same as *victory*; *hesitation, pause* and *popularity, fame* are not linked to the word *victory*; *defeat* and *loss* are opposite to *victory*.
3	Tick the correct box.	**defeat, loss** ✔
4	Check your answer.	

✏ Try this

1 Match the **synonyms**.

determination	spoil
investigate	check
fake	agree
corrupt	fraudulent
comply	persistence

2 Write **antonyms** for the words below.

illuminate _____

tragic _____

scarce _____

contemporary _____

★ Top tip

- Remember: *S* for synonym, *S* for same. *A* for antonym, *A* for against (opposite to).

SPELLING

Word families

To achieve the higher score, you need to know words which share the same root word or prefix.

★ What you need to know

- Many words are related in form and meaning; these are known as **word families**.
- Words that belong to a family usually share the same root word or prefix. For example: *sign signature design; auto automatic autobiography autonomous; science scientific; conscience unconscious*

★ Let's practise

Circle three words that belong to the same **word family**.
antiseptic antisocial sobriety society sociable soccer

1	Read the question and read it again. What is it asking?	The question is asking you to find words with a common root word.
2	Which parts of words are repeated?	*anti* is repeated twice. *iety* is repeated twice. *so* is repeated five times.
3	Check the *so* words to find a longer pattern.	*sob* is used once, *soc* is used four times, *soci* is used three times. It may be *soci*.
4	Check that the words you have chosen share a meaning.	*antisocial*, *society* and *sociable* all contain the idea of being about people.
5	Check your answer.	antiseptic (antisocial) sobriety (society) (sociable) soccer

✎ Try this

1 Add two more words to this **word family**.

   create _____ _____

2 Underline the two words that belong to the **word family** of <u>mal</u>, meaning bad.

   mallard   male   maltreat   malicious   malted

Word list for Years 5 and 6

Top tips
- Learn a few spellings each day.
- Use the look, cover, say and write method.
- Write sentences using these words.
- Look at the words and find other words within them (e.g. *independent* contains *in*, *depend*, *pen*, *dent*).
- Create exaggerated pronunciations for some of them (e.g. *in- de- pen- dent*).
- Look for patterns or properties (for example, many contain double letters).

accommodate	embarrass	persuade
accompany	environment	physical
according	equip (*-ped*, *-ment*)	prejudice
achieve	especially	privilege
aggressive	exaggerate	profession
amateur	excellent	programme
ancient	existence	pronunciation
apparent	explanation	queue
appreciate	familiar	recognise
attached	foreign	recommend
available	forty	relevant
average	frequently	restaurant
awkward	government	rhyme
bargain	guarantee	rhythm
bruise	harass	sacrifice
category	hindrance	secretary
cemetery	identity	shoulder
committee	immediate(ly)	signature
communicate	individual	sincere(ly)
community	interfere	soldier
competition	interrupt	stomach
conscience	language	sufficient
conscious	leisure	suggest
controversy	lightning	symbol
convenience	marvellous	system
correspond	mischievous	temperature
criticise (*critic* + *ise*)	muscle	thorough
curiosity	necessary	twelfth
definite	neighbour	variety
desperate	nuisance	vegetable
determined	occupy	vehicle
develop	occur	yacht
dictionary	opportunity	
disastrous	parliament	

Glossary

Abstract noun A word that gives a name to a concept (e.g. beauty) rather than an object (e.g. table).
Active voice The sentence form that uses subject + verb order.
Adjective A word that describes a noun.
Adverb A word that adds information to a verb.
Adverbial A word or a group of words that adds information about a verb.
Antonym A word that is an opposite of another.
Apostrophe A punctuation mark that is used to replace a letter in a contracted word, or to indicate possession.
Auxiliary verb A verb used with another verb to give information about its tense. Auxiliary verbs are: 'be', 'have', 'do' and modal verbs.
Bullet point A punctuation mark used to identify items in a vertical list.
Capital letter An upper case letter.
Colon A punctuation mark that is used to introduce a list or an explanation or conclusion.
Comma A punctuation mark that is used to separate clauses within a sentence, or items in a list.
Conjunction A word or phrase that is used to join two clauses within a sentence.
Contraction A word that consists of two words in a shortened form, e.g. do not = don't.
Coordinating conjunction A word that joins one main clause to another main clause.
Dash A punctuation mark that can be used singly to introduce a dependent clause or phrase, or in pairs to indicate parenthesis.
Determiner A word which introduces a noun, e.g. a, the.
Exclamation Starts with 'How' or 'What' and includes a verb.
Exclamation mark A punctuation mark that indicates an emotional expression, e.g. shock, delight.
Fronted adverbial An adverbial that has been moved before the verb. It is often followed by a comma.
Full stop A punctuation mark that indicates the end of a sentence.
Homophone A word whose pronunciation has more than one meaning, e.g. hear, here.
Hyphen A symbol of punctuation that is used to combine two words, e.g. quick-minded.
Inverted commas Punctuation marks, also called speech marks, that are used to indicate direct speech.
Main clause A part of a sentence that is not dependent upon other parts of the sentence to make sense.
Modal verb A word that is used in combination with another verb to indicate probability or obligation.
Noun A word that describes an object or abstract idea.
Noun phrase A group of words which give information about and are dependent upon the noun.
Object A word or words that refer to the person or thing to which a verb is done.
Parenthesis A part of a sentence that contains information that is not integral to the meaning of that sentence.
Passive voice A sentence type in which the subject of the verb is not known, or not important and so the action or object of the verb become the focus.

Past perfect tense A verb form often used to make comparison between events in the historic past, prior to an event in the more recent past, e.g. He had opened the box before I could stop him.
Past progressive tense A verb form composed of the verb 'be' and a verb form ending in -ing to indicate an action that happened continuously in the past, e.g. I was running.
Personal pronoun A word used to replace the name of a person or object in relation to a verb.
Possessive pronoun A word used to replace the name of a person or object to which something belongs.
Prefix Letters that are added to the start of a root word to change the meaning or form.
Preposition A word that indicates place or time; it is used within a noun phrase.
Present perfect A verb form that refers to an action begun in the past and continuing to the present.
Present progressive tense A verb form composed of the verb 'be' and a verb form ending in -ing to indicate an action that happens continuously in the present.
Present tense Verb forms that describe actions that happen in the present.
Pronoun A word that is used to substitute a noun.
Punctuation The symbols used to indicate the structure of sentences.
Question mark A punctuation mark used to indicate that a sentence is a question.
Relative clause A group of words, including a verb, that provide information about a noun.
Relative pronoun A word that connects a clause to a noun or pronoun, e.g. My sister who lives in ….
Semi-colon A punctuation mark that is used to connect two closely related ideas, acting as a bridge between two related sentences.
Silent letter A letter that is used within the spelling of a word, but whose sound is not pronounced.
Speech mark See *Inverted commas*.
Subject A word or words that indicate the person or thing performing the verb in a sentence.
Subjunctive verb form A verb form that is used to indicate the hypothetical nature of a verb, or to demonstrate formality.
Subordinate clause A group of words, including a verb, that is dependent upon the main clause in a sentence.
Subordinating conjunction A word or phrase that is used to introduce a subordinate clause.
Suffix A letter or letters that are added to the end of a word; it usually changes the word form, e.g. verb to noun: forgive – forgiveness.
Synonym A word that has the same, or very similar, meaning to another word.
Verb A word, or words, that describe an action or state.
Verb form The term used to refer to the different ways in which a verb may be used, e.g. running, ran, has run.
Word family A group of words that has a common feature or pattern.

Answers

Nouns (page 8)
1. circle: ideas
2. Accept answers that change the word *suggestion* to a suitable alternative that makes sense, e.g. writing; dancing; idea; speech.

Adjectives (page 9)
1. circle: sticky; spilled; runny; happy
2. Accept a sentence that makes sense and changes the words *disappointed* and *last* to more positive adjectives, e.g. disappointed = happy, triumphant, satisfied; last = first, best.

Adverbs (page 10)
1. Accept answers that change the word *fast* and make sense, e.g. loudly; quickly; quietly.
2. circle: soon; straight; hard

Modal verbs (page 11)
1. Accept the use of a modal verb that expresses greater possibility than 'might', e.g. He *can*; *will*; *should*; *could* win the race today.
2. Accept any suitable modal verb, e.g. may; might. Answers must be correctly spelt.

Adverbials (page 13)
1. circle: in the river
2. tick: Before the start of the film, let's get some popcorn.
   I'll give you some money to buy ice-creams for everyone.
3. Accept answers that make sense and contain an adverbial, e.g. every day; on the school field.
4. Accept answers with correct use of capital letters and comma: Before going to the dentist, Aisling brushed her teeth.
5. Accept answers that refer to the adverbial explaining *where* the party is, e.g. It shows where the party is.
6. tick: The class would go bug hunting in the woods after lunch.
   Please put the books on the table before you leave.
   Would you like a drink before supper?

Pronouns (page 15)
1. Mr White was tidying his classroom. pronoun
   I can't believe that he won. pronoun
   The children were playing outside. no pronoun
   Their kittens were asleep in the bed. no pronoun
2. Where is mine? possessive
   Jane, who was the oldest, took care of everyone. relative
   She didn't believe the story. personal
3. circle: I; our; them; My; I; my; her
4. He went to her house.
5. tick: it its my
6. Accept answers that refer to the substitution of *She* for *Jessica*, e.g. It is instead of saying *Jessica* twice. / *She* is used to avoid beginning each sentence with the girl's name.

Prepositions (page 17)
1. underline: beneath; in; between
2. We left the restaurant before dessert. preposition
   Tickets to enter the theme park are more expensive before 11 in the morning. preposition.
   We have breakfast before we leave for school. subordinating conjuction
3. Accept any suitable prepositions that make sense across the whole sentence. For example: After; Before; At/on; beside; below; under; beneath / in.
4. Accept any suitable preposition that makes sense, e.g. Oscar placed the package *below*; *beside*; *beneath*; *above*; *next to* the table.
5. between/opposite; beside/opposite; beside; opposite/on

Determiners (page 19)
1. tick: Do you like these pictures?
   These games are my favourites.
2. some; any; the
3. some; these/any; the/this; that
4. underline: This; an; some; more
5. the; a/any; many/a
6. tick: Please pass those biscuits.
   Can I have this chair please?
   My favourite is this one.
7. circle: A; that; The; the; some

Subordinating and coordinating conjunctions (page 21)
1. circle: while; but; and
2. unless
3. although; but; even though/if; when; as soon as. Answers must be correctly spelt.
4. underline: Unless; and; when
5. After we have been swimming, let's have a hot chocolate. subordinating conjunction
   Can you collect the newspaper after breakfast? preposition
   Shall we have one last dive before we get out of the pool? subordinating conjunction
   Henry will be in Scotland until January. preposition
   Jasmin can play with us until her sister comes to collect her. subordinating conjunction
6. even though; when; because

Main clauses and subordinate clauses (page 23)
1. underline: that require very clean water in which to live; since rivers have become less polluted
2. unless; Although; when; that
3. Accept any suitable subordinate clause that makes sense (this must include a verb), e.g. you go to work.
4. underline: My favourite cousin; is coming to visit.
5. tick: Birds puff up their feathers when the weather is very cold.
   If you feed the birds in your garden, they will visit you regularly.

Relative clauses (page 25)
1. circle: who lives in Canada
2. tick: The wind blasted through the door that Kate had left open.
   The trees that Tom planted last year were growing well.
3. Accept any suitable relative clause that makes sense, e.g. I have moved the books *which belong to the library*; *that were on the table*.
4. which; when; where
5. tick: The girl who lives on my Gran's street is in my class.

Noun phrases (page 26)
1. underline: The oak tree at the end of the garden
2. Accept any suitable answer that expands *Susie* or *skills*, e.g. My big sister, Susie, .../ Susie is proud of her outstanding; growing basketball skills.
3. circle: The evening wind; the creaking trees; a ghostly noise

Subject and object (page 27)
1. circle: the guitar; breakfast; our cousin's house. underline: Joshua; Yuri; We

Subject and verb agreement (page 29)
1. circle: is; are
2. circle: is; are; is; is
3. tick: Most pupils are keen to help with the concert.
   The library is closed.
4. Accept: David *buys*; *bought*; *is buying*; *will buy*; *has bought*; *had bought* a book.
5. Accept any suitable explanation, e.g. the verb does not fit with the subject; cousin does not fit with 'come'; the word (verb) should be 'comes' not 'come'.
6. circle: were; were; was

Verbs in the progressive and perfect tenses (page 31)
1. Daniel is making dinner this evening. present progressive
   Lucy has made drinks for all the party guests. present perfect
   The children are lining up for lunch. present progressive
   We had arrived on time but the others were late. present perfect
2. underline: was raining; was shining
3. Accept any suitable verb in the present perfect form that makes sense, e.g. has lived; has grown up; has been.
4. The twins have learned; learnt to play dominoes today.
5. had made

Passive and active voices (page 33)
1. Last night, trees were knocked over by the wind. passive
   My brother loves watching cowboy films. active
   My boots were chewed by our dogs. passive
   Oscar designed a super castle. active
2. The football match was won by our school.
3. The children ate the cake.
4. The whales were feeding on a school of fish. active
   The fish had been trapped in a net. passive
   The boats were followed by dolphins. passive
   Dolphins are sometimes caught in fishing nets. passive
5. Accept answers which refer to passive voice putting emphasis on what is done rather than who is doing it, e.g. it is not important who does the action/warms the test tube.

Subjunctive verb forms (page 35)
1. circle: join
2. underline: make
3. tick: If I were you, I would practise my guitar a little more often.
   If you recommend that he study harder, he will do it.

ANSWERS

4 were
5 eat
6 tick: I wish Ben were here as he would know what to do.
Lola insisted that her sister help with the washing up.

Standard English and formality (page 37)
1 Ed hasn't got any more money left.
2 ascertain; endeavour; attend; accompany
3 Alex has done; did fewer lengths of the pool than me.
4 fewer; less; fewer; fwer

Capital letters, full stops, exclamation marks and question marks (page 39)
1 How interesting that was!
What would you like to do?
Although you're late, it's great to see you.
2 The door opened suddenly and the class all turned to look. The special guest had arrived. Everyone had been looking forward to this moment.
3 At Heathton School, our classes learn Spanish and French.
Accept answers that refer to proper nouns, e.g. Heathton/School: A capital letter is used because it is (part of) a name (of a place). Spanish/French: A capital letter is used because it is a name of a language.
At: A capital letter is used because it is the start of the sentence.
4 Accept answers that refer to surprise or disappointment. Answers should refer to the sentence starting with What and including a verb.
5 I had never seen such a strange creature. Whatever could it be? Living in Spain was turning out to be full of surprises.
6 underline: london; tuesday; downing street; prime minister

Commas (page 41)
1 Although Alma loves hamsters, mice and rats, she doesn't like gerbils.
2 Quickly, before it rains, run inside.
3 My favourite desserts are strawberry and vanilla ice-cream, apple pie with custard and fresh fruit salad.
4 I will tell, Jake.
5 Accept answers that explain how one sentence is about Susie and the other is addressed to her, e.g. The first sentence is about the girl, and the second one is talking to her.
6 I play tennis, which is my favourite sport, at the weekends.
7 tick: Two cars, a red one and a green one, were racing side by side.
Trains, especially high-speed ones, are a comfortable way to travel.

Inverted commas (page 43)
1 tick: Mrs Archer asked, "Which city is the capital of France?"
2 "Please sit down here," requested the dentist.
3 "My brother is a champion chess player," boasted Archie.
Lucia replied, "My sister wins competitions too."
4 "We won the match,"/"We won the match!" shouted the team excitedly.
5 "Do you know how to play chess?"
6 "I will tidy my room," promised Jake, "after I finish this game."

Apostrophes (page 45)
1 a) the boat's mast   d) the rivers' mouths
  b) the sailors' hats   e) today's sunshine
  c) the river's source   f) last week's rain

2 he wouldn't; she'll; you mustn't. Answers must be correctly spelt.
3 didn't; it'd; hadn't
4 They've reached the mountain's peak and planted the group's flag on the very top.
5 Accept answers that refer to the function of the apostrophe, e.g. pupils': An apostrophe is used to show that the books belong to the pupils.
weren't: An apostrophe is used to show that a letter is missing.

Parenthesis (page 46)
1 tick: Jena always has her favourite breakfast – toast and ice-cream – on Sundays.
2 My sister (much to my surprise) gave me a present.
3 Accept answers that refer to parenthesis including non-essential/extra information.

Colons, semi-colons, single dashes, hyphens and bullet points (page 47)
1 Whenever I see you, you make me smile; you are my very best friend.
2 It should not have happened – in my opinion.
3 I eat a lot of fruit: apples, oranges, plums.

Prefixes and suffixes (page 48)
1 conscious   unconscious(ness/ly), subconscious(ness/ly)
  standard   substandard(ly)
  forgive   forgive(ness)
  believe   disbelieve
  judge   judgement
  commence   recommence(ment)
  thought   unthoughtful(ness)
2 circle: mis
3 swift<u>est</u>; fruit<u>less</u>; aware<u>ness</u>; pay<u>ment</u>

Prefixes (page 49)
1 incapable; income; precaution; anti-social; dissimilar; illogical
2 in: advisable
  im: measurable; plausible; perfection
  il: logical; legitimate
  ir: relevant; regularity
3 a) intercity   d) autobiography
  b) antibiotic   e) subconscious
  c) subnormal   f) supernatural

Suffixes: -tion, -ssion, -cian (page 50)
1 t; d; te
2 electrician; musician; optician; politician

Suffixes: -ous, -tious, -cious (page 51)
1 mysterious; studious; glorious
2 gracious; spacious
3 -eous: advantageous; hideous; courteous; simultaneous
  -ious: cautious; hilarious; delicious; curious; precious; devious
  -tious: cautious; ambitious; infectious

Suffixes: -able, -ably, -ible, -ibly (page 52)
1 -able/-ably: adorably; applicable; unnoticeable; understandably; probably; reasonable; reachable; irrevocable; comfortable
  -ible/-ibly: horrible; invisibly; accessible; intelligible
2 pity: pitiable; pitiably
  avoid: avoidable; avoidably
  believe: believable; believably
  classify: classifiable; classifiably

Suffixes: -ant, -ance, -ancy, -ent, -ence, -ency (page 53)
1 -ent, -ence, -ency: audience; experiences; audience; tendency; confidence; competence
  -ant, -ance, -ancy: performance; circumstances; disturbance; hesitant; balance
2 a) obedient   b) persistent

Words with ei, eigh, ey, ay (page 54)
1 a) neighbour   b) sleigh

Words with ie, ei (page 54)
1 a) weird   d) forfeit
  b) foreign   e) retrieval
  c) sovereign   f) obedience

Words with ough (page 55)
1 a) ought   b) toughest
2 Accept answers that give approximate definitions as below:
  borough   a named area within a city
  bough   part of a tree; another word for a branch
  doughnut   a type of sweet cooked cake
  drought   a period of time without rainfall

Word endings: al, el, il, le (page 56)
1 a) muddle   f) sprinkle
  b) pummel   g) kennel
  c) icicle   h) arable
  d) flannel   i) carousel
  e) incredible
2 a) classical   d) archaeological
  b) functional   e) professional
  c) educational f) medical

Silent letters (page 57)
1 b doubt; tomb; debt
  d Wednesday
  h anchor; stomach; chrome
  k knell; knead; knuckle
  n solemn
  p psychology; receipt
  t glisten; hustle
  u guitar
  w wrist; wretch; sword
2 a thumb (circle 'b')
  b knuckle (circle 'k')
  c tongue (circle 'ue')
  d wrist (circle 'w')
  e stomach (circle 'h')
  f knee (circle 'k')
3 underline: Wednesday; sword; receipt; doubt; chrome; glistened; sunlight; wrist; ache

Homophones (page 58)
1 a) stationary   e) accept
  b) stationery   f) except
  c) course   g) affect
  d) coarse   h) effect

Synonyms and antonyms (page 59)
1 determination   persistence
  investigate   check
  fake   fraudulent
  corrupt   spoil
  comply   agree
2 Accept answers that offer suitable antonyms, e.g.
  illuminate: darken
  tragic: happy, funny
  scarce: plentiful, common
  contemporary: old, antique

Word families (page 60)
1 any two words from: creation, creative, creature
2 underline: maltreat, malicious